A FIRST NUMBER BOOK

Platt & Munk , Publishers/New York

A Division of Grosset & Dunlap

A FIRST NUMBER BOOK

By Shari Robinson

Pictures by Sal Murdocca

To Ruth and Herta.

With special thanks to Beth Teitelman
for her assistance.

Library of Congress Catalog Number: 80-83587
ISBN: 0-448-47335-6 (Trade Edition)
ISBN: 0-448-13922-7 (Library Edition)
Copyright © 1975 by Platt & Munk Publishers.
Copyright © 1981 by Grosset & Dunlap, Inc.
All rights reserved.
Published simultaneously in Canada. Printed in the United States of America.
(Originally published as *Numbers, Signs, and Pictures: A First Number Book.*)

Mark Skiber

Contents

8

Numbers: A Code For How Many

Sometimes we want to show how many things we have.
We may have a lot of things. Or we may have a few.
Suppose we want to show how many paint brushes we have.
We could draw this picture 🖌🖌🖌
to show we have this many.
But it would take a long time to draw
each paint brush.
What if we invented symbols to show
how many things we have?
It would be a code.
This symbol 4 would show that we have
this many 🖌🖌🖌🖌 paint brushes.
And this symbol 2 would show that we have
only this many 🖌🖌 paint brushes.
Then we could look at our symbols
and know right away how many paint brushes we have.
Many years ago, people invented symbols to show
just how many things they had.
These symbols are called numbers.
Each number has a name that can be spelled.
Sometimes we spell the name instead of writing the symbol.
This symbol 4 is spelled this way: four.

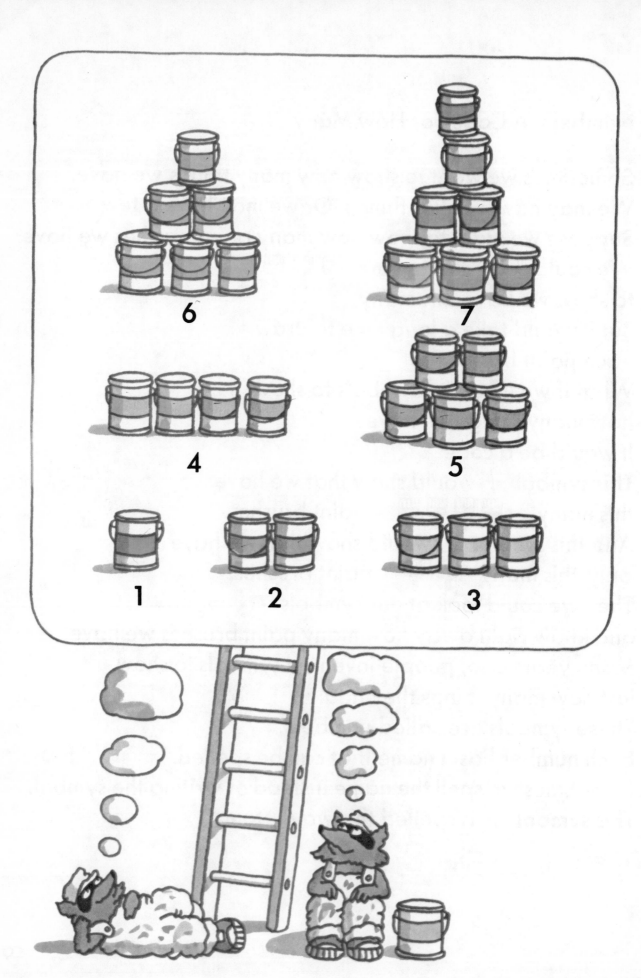

Counting Tells Us How Many

We find out just how many things we have
by counting.
Counting tells us the number of things
in any kind of group or collection.
We can even count a collection of letters.
Let us count the number of letters in
the word COUNT.
C is one. O is two. U is three. N is four. And
T is five. There are five letters in the word "count."
When we first learn to count, we count one thing at a time.
If we count a stack of six paint cans, we count one
paint can at a time.
One good thing about numbers is that each
number always stands for the same amount.
Three is this many paint cans 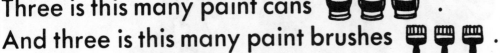 .
And three is this many paint brushes .

ONE RHINO RHUMBAS

2

TWO TOOTHLESS TIGERS

THREE FAT FISH

FOUR FOXES FEELING FOXY

FIVE GENTLEMEN JOGGING

SIX WALRUSES WASHING

SEVEN SORRY SNAKES

EIGHT PUMPKINS PEDALING

NINE KNIGHTS IN A NET

TEN TEAPOTS TOOTING

Numbers Put Things In Order

Numbers can tell us exactly where a
thing is placed in a collection.
They can tell us in just what order
each thing belongs.
When we count the steps on a ladder,
the first step is one.
The second step is two.
The third step is three.
When we watch a race, we count each
racer as he gets to the finish line.
We count the first to come in, the
second to come in, the third to come in,
and so on.
This is how numbers bring order to things.

Rats Racing

The results of a rat race

What We Count

What things do we count?
We count things that are in a group
or collection. Usually these things
are similar in some way.
We can count the number of people in
a family, or the number of train cars on
a track, or the number of animals in a
zoo.
We can count a collection of five ladders,
and a collection of two painters.
But we cannot count the painters and ladders
in one collection. If we did so, we would have
to say that there are seven ladders and painters,
and this would be wrong.
Sometimes a collection is made up of things
that are not all in the same position.
If there is a collection of five ladders,
and one ladder is lying down, there still
is a collection of five ladders.
But if one ladder is put away in the basement,
a new collection of four ladders is formed.
A collection can be small. And a
collection can be large.
There can even be two collections of the
same things.
A collection is sometimes called a set.

Two telephones have a terrific time
talking to each other.

Eight radios have a terrible time
talking to each other.

**All the alligators belong to
Alligator's Rocktime Band.**

even if they are placed differently.

**Even the bad bear belongs to
the Bear Brigade.**

Six
weightlifters
lifting weights.

If a member is removed, a new collection is made.

One
weightlifter
takes a walk.

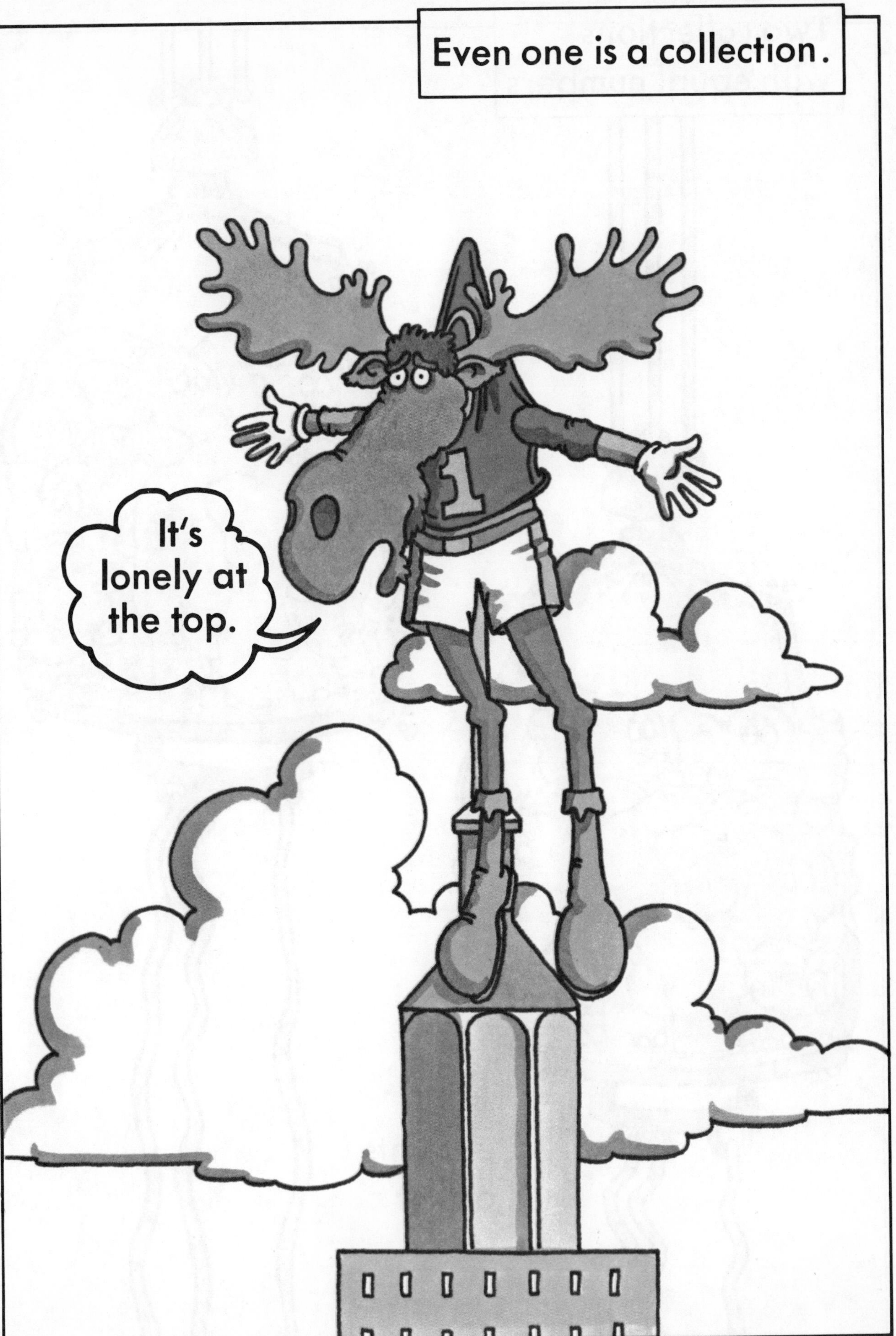
Even one is a collection.
It's lonely at the top.

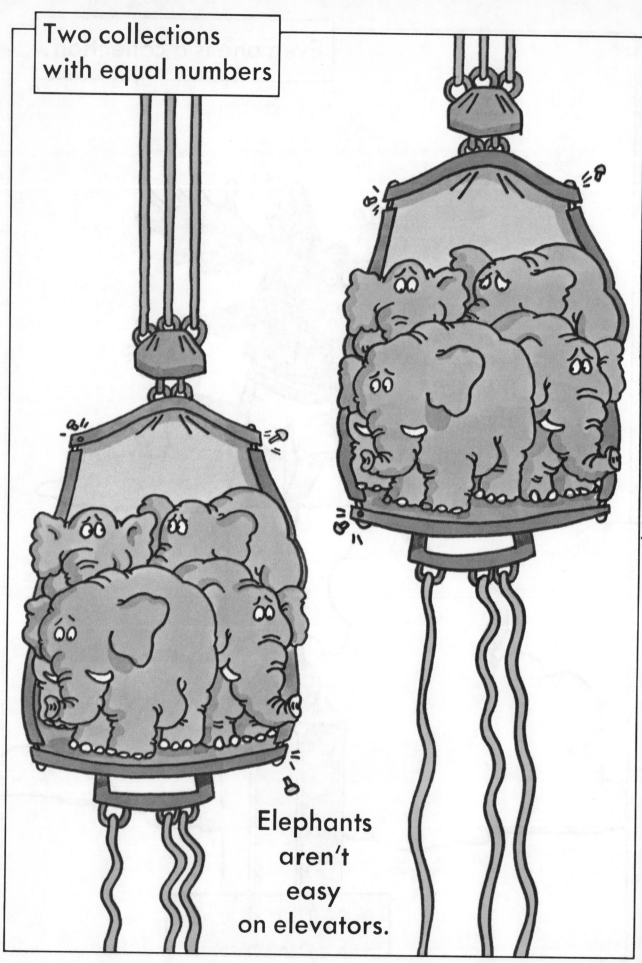

Elephants
aren't
easy
on elevators.

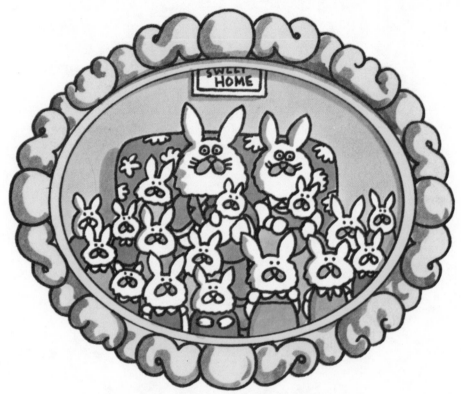

Regular rabbit family

Rare rabbit family

What is Zero?

Just as one is a number, and two is a number,
zero is a number.
Zero also tells us how many things are
in a collection.
Zero tells us that there are no things
in a collection.
If we want to know how many quarts of paint
are in a bucket, and the bucket is empty,
then there are zero quarts of paint in the bucket.
The symbol that we use for zero is ○ .

Sequence Counting: Counting More Than One At A Time

We do not always have to count one thing at a time.
We can count two things at a time,
or three things at a time,
or four things at a time.
But each time, we must count the same number
of things at a time.
If we climb up two steps at a time,
we start with zero, and add two, then add two again
and again....
We count two, four, six, eight, ten.
If toy soldiers are marching three in a row,
we add three each time: three, six, nine.
Counting this way is called sequence counting.

Two cowboys kicked out

Four cowboys kicked out

Kicked out cowboys can't kick up a fuss.

Six cowboys kicked out

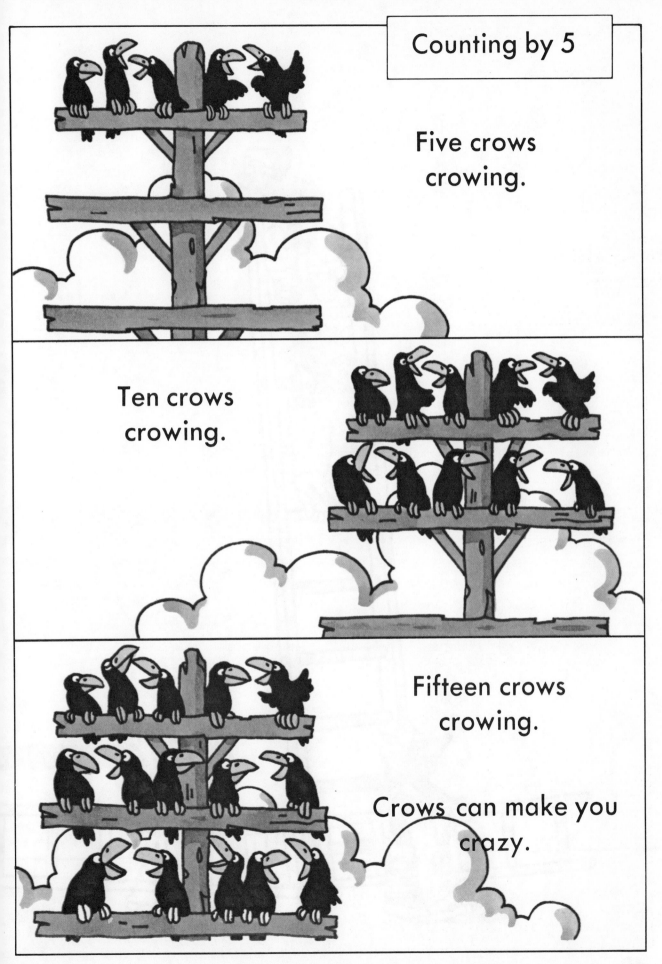

Counting by 5

Five crows
crowing.

Ten crows
crowing.

Fifteen crows
crowing.

Crows can make you
crazy.

41

42

What is Addition?

Addition is like counting.
Addition is adding the number of things
in one collection to the number of things
in another collection. Then you have a
new collection.
If we count two painters standing on a ladder,
and we then count two more painters walking
by the ladder,
we have counted four painters.
In addition, this sign + is called the plus sign.
It is placed between the two numbers which are
added together.
And this sign = is called the equal sign.
It is placed after the two numbers which are
added together. The number after
the equal sign shows the number of things
in the new collection.

$1+0=1$

One lonely ghost

One lonely ghost has no luck looking.

One lonely ghost keeps looking.

Two ghosts get together.

2+1=3

1+2=3

Two pigs and one pig pull.

One pig and two pigs pull.

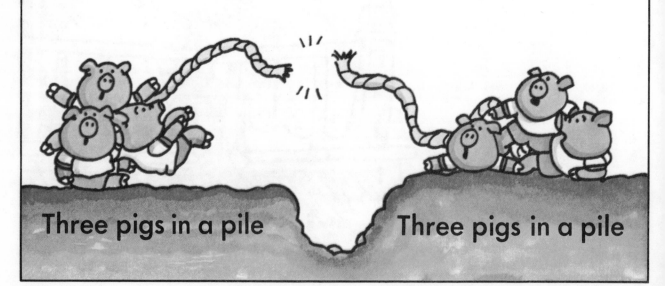

Three pigs in a pile

Three pigs in a pile

2+2=4

Two sad sacks sobbing.

Two sad sacks sniffling.

Singing puts sad sacks in sharp shape.

2 + 3 = 5

Two
hippos

haul

three hippos
by helicopter.

Five hippos are hard for one helicopter to handle.

3+3=6

Three whales who watch their weight

Three whales who watch their weight

Six whales can break a scale.

49

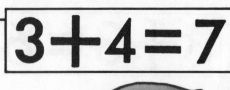

3+4=7

Three chipmunks carry a cello.

Four chums help the three chipmunks.

Seven chipmunks play a cello concerto.

Six hops and that goose's goose is cooked.

For more
adventures in
THE WILD
GOOSE CHASE
see page 64.

51

$$5+5=10$$

Five butterflies

flutter by

five other butterflies.

Ten butterflies become a
Butterfly Ballet.

What is Subtraction?

Subtraction tells us how much of a difference
there is between two numbers.
In subtraction, we remove part of the
collection from the whole collection.
This way we learn what the difference
is between the whole collection and
part of the collection.
The first number we use in subtraction
is the number which shows how many things
are in the whole collection.
The second number shows how many things
are being taken away from the collection.
In between these numbers we put this sign: —.
This is called the minus sign.
In subtraction, the number after the equal sign
shows what the difference between
the two collections is.

$10 - 0 = 10$

Ten mice make a mess.

$10 - 1 = 9$

One mouse goes for mops.

Nine mice make a mess.

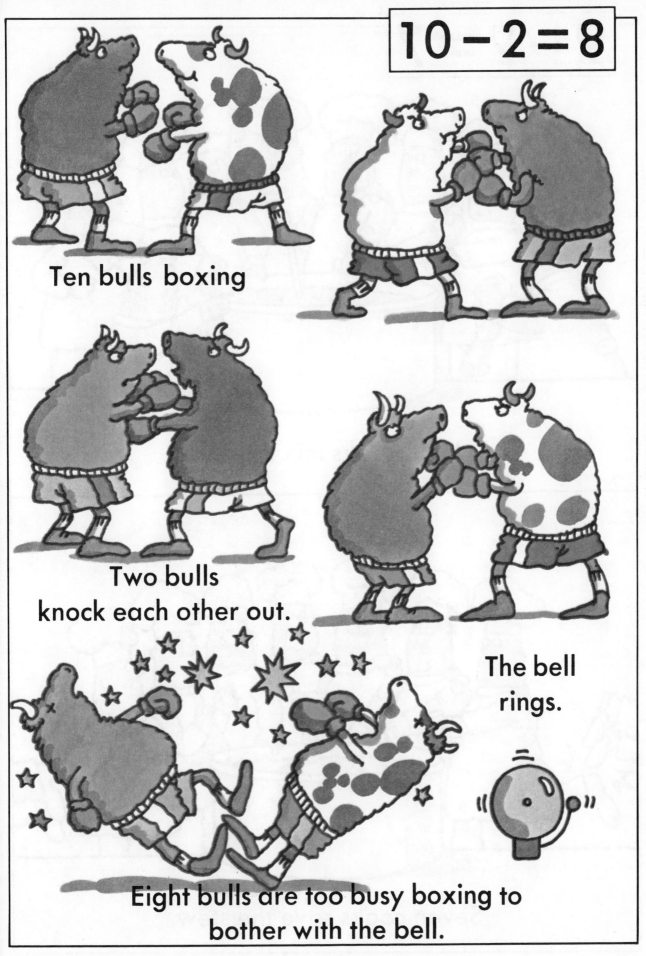

$$10 - 2 = 8$$

Ten bulls boxing

Two bulls knock each other out.

The bell rings.

Eight bulls are too busy boxing to bother with the bell.

9 - 2 = 7

Nine cooks mix a brew.

Seven cooks save the stew.

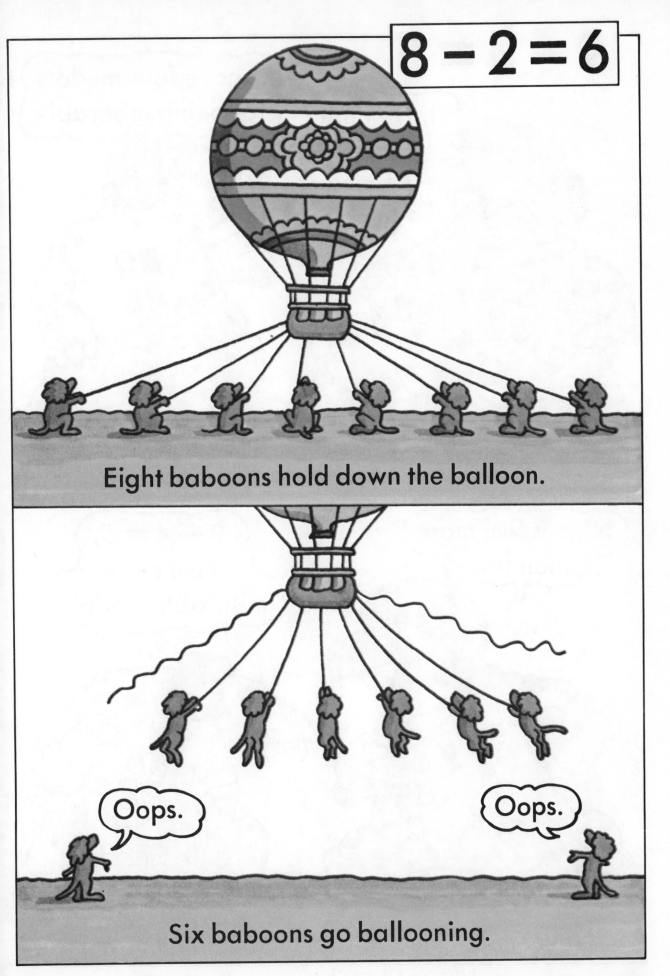

8 − 2 = 6

Eight baboons hold down the balloon.

Six baboons go ballooning.

59

Never mind. Medals don't make the monster.

Bird balances nine books

Bird balances four books

Bird balances no books

3+3=6

Three watchmen wonder.

Six watchmen wonder who is watching whom.

$$6 - 3 = 3$$

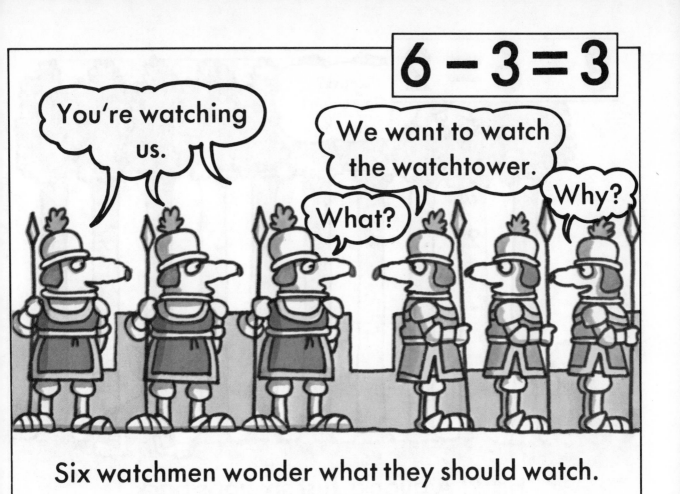

Six watchmen wonder what they should watch.

Three watchmen still wonder.

Hark! A quack! Just six hops back.

For more adventures in THE WILD GOOSE CHASE see page 73

64

4 − 3 = 1

Four toads talk about a torn tent.

Three toads take tent to Tentmender.

A toad who only talks about trouble talks to himself.

What Is Multiplication?

Multiplication is like addition.
But in multiplication, we add only
collections with equal numbers of
things in them.
If we are putting together
several equal collections, we are
making a new collection, just as in addition.
Multiplication is a short cut to addition.
Let us say that we want to combine three
groups of two painters into one big group.
We would add two painters + two painters
+ two painters.
Or instead, we could multiply three times
two painters.
They both equal six.
In multiplication, this sign ✕ is called
the times sign. It means " times the amount of ."
It shows us how many times a number is being
multiplied.
In multiplication, we also find
that one thing might be
twice as large as another.
It might also be half as large.

2+2+2=6

  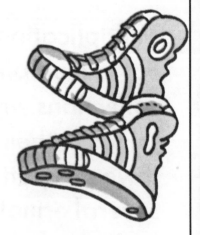

| Two sneakers sneaking snooping sneezing. | Two sneakers snooping sneezing sneaking. | Two sneakers sneezing snooping sneaking. |

Six sneaking, snooping, sneezing sneakers

Three pairs of sneakers,
snooping, sneaking,
and sneezing.

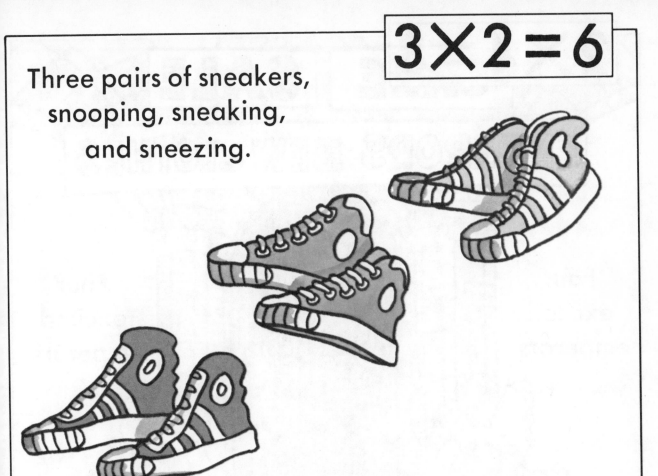

Six sneaking, snooping, sneezing sneakers

Eight excited emperors enter a sale.

3×3=9

Three spies

Three spies

Three spies

Nine spies spy on each other.

Twice

One tall troll is twice as tall as one small troll.

Two small trolls are just as tall as one tall troll.

Half

**Two small trolls
are half as tall as two tall trolls.**

What Is Division?

Division is like subtraction.
In division, we start out with
a whole collection, and split up
the collection into equal parts.
In division, we ask, into how many parts
can a collection be equally divided,
and how many numbers are in each
part.
The first number in a division problem shows
how many are in the whole collection.
The second number shows how many parts
it is to be divided into.
In division this sign $\div$ means that
we are splitting the collection into
equal parts.
$6 \div 3$ means a collection of six
is being divided into three equal parts.
The number after the equal sign shows
how many things are in each part.

Two rug bugs at a ring rack

Three bakers bake three cakes.

Nine cakes on a cake counter

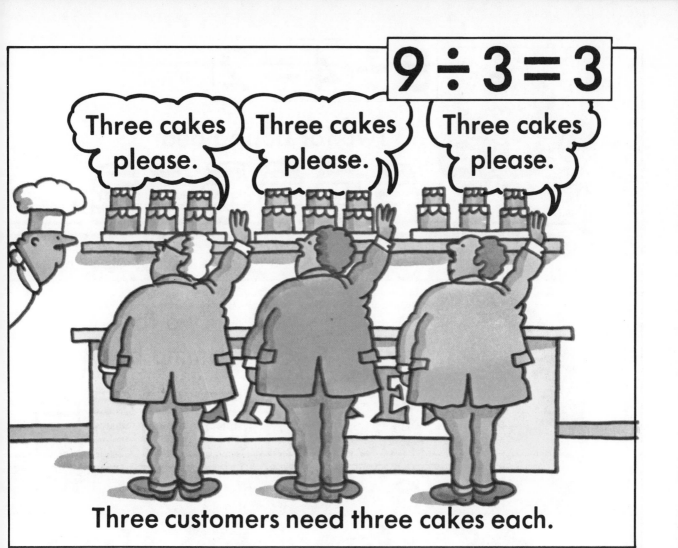

Three customers need three cakes each.

Three customers each carry off three cakes.

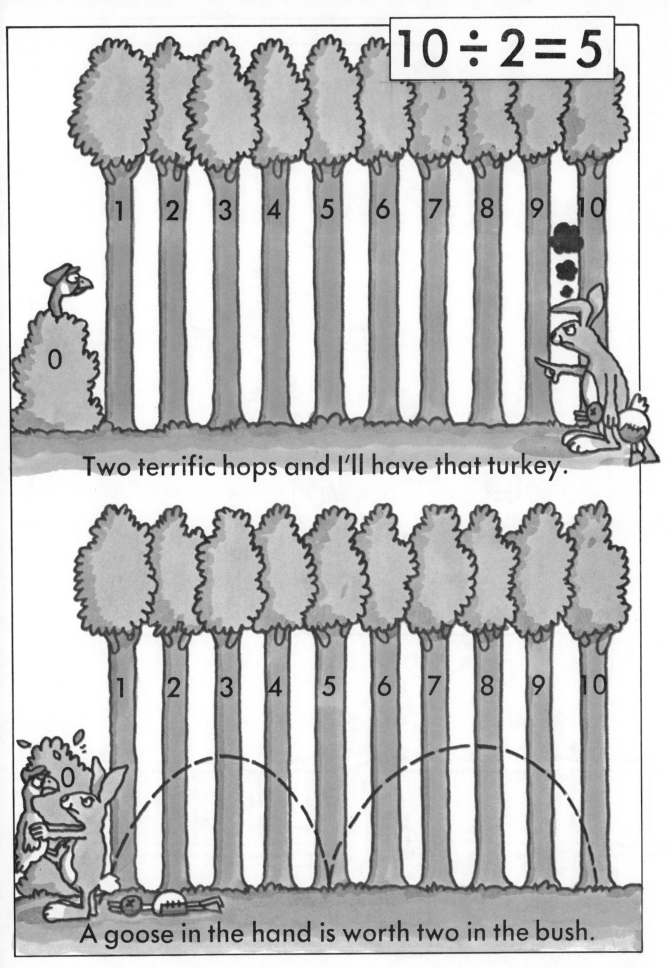

10 ÷ 2 = 5

0   1   2   3   4   5   6   7   8   9   10

Two terrific hops and I'll have that turkey.

0   1   2   3   4   5   6   7   8   9   10

A goose in the hand is worth two in the bush.

Ten and Over

There are so many things to count,
that it is hard to have a different symbol
for each number of things. So, we combine
the numbers in a special way.
A long time ago, when people wanted to keep
track of things, they counted with pebbles.
They figured out a way of putting the pebbles
in columns.
In the first column, each pebble stood for one
of each thing they were counting.
Once they reached 10, they started a new
column and each pebble in that column stood
for 10 of each thing.
In the next column, each pebble stood for
one hundred of each thing.
Take the number 125. The 5 stands for
the number of ones. There are five ones.
The 2 stands for the number of tens.
There are two tens.
The 1 stands for the number of hundreds.
There is one hundred.

Ten totems on totem poles

Fifteen totems on totem poles

Twenty totems on totem poles

Twenty - five totems on totem poles

Fifty totems...

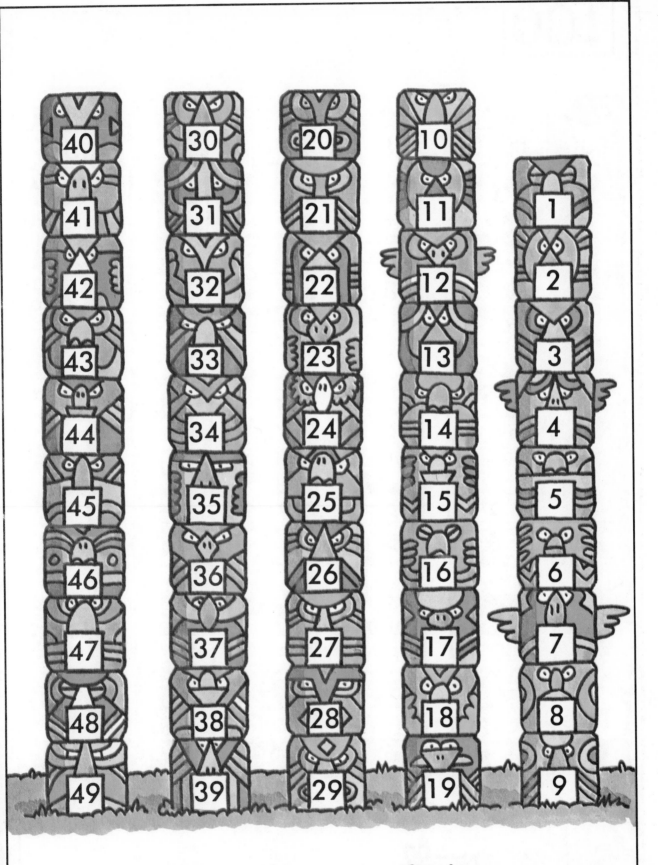

on totem poles are terrific, but . . .

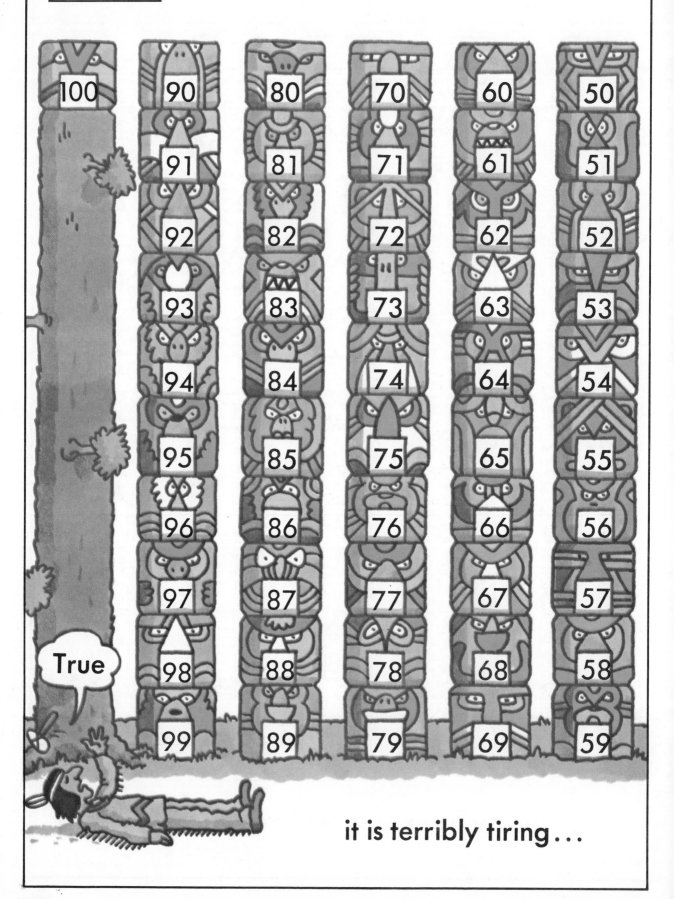

100

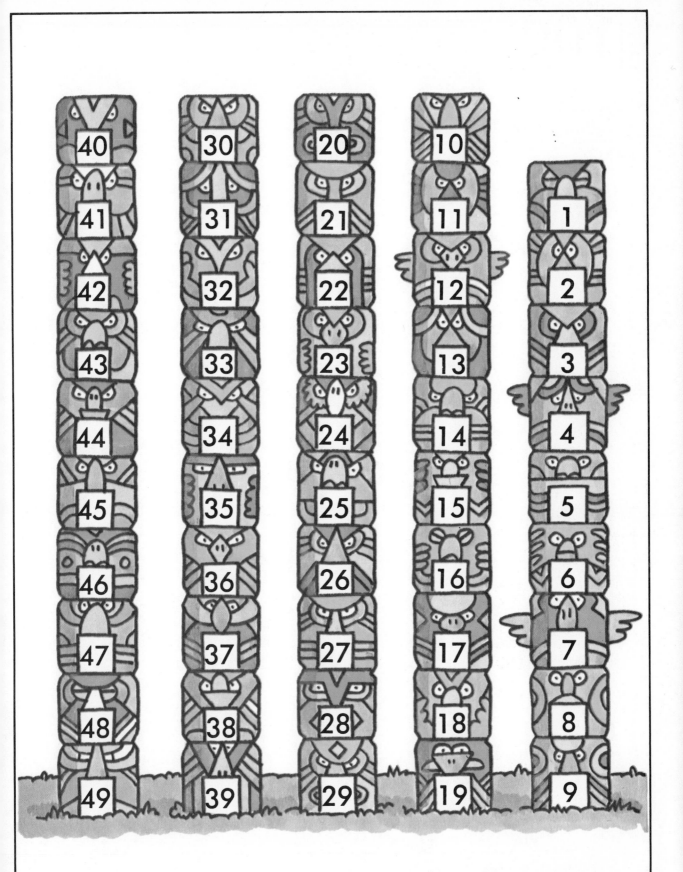

making one hundred totems on totem poles.

The End